A QUARTERLY DAY BOOK

WITH PROMPTS AND TOOLS

NIMBLE BOOKS LLC

Nimble Books LLC

1521 Martha Avenue

Ann Arbor, MI, USA 48103

http://www.NimbleBooks.com

wfz@nimblebooks.com

+1.734-330-2593

Version 1.0; last saved 2011-02-21.

Printed in the United States of America

The paper used in this publication meets the minimum requirements of the American National Standard for Information Sciences—Permanence of Paper for Printed Library Materials, ANSI Z39.48-1992. The paper is acid-free and lignin-free.

Day _____ Month _____ Day ___ Year _____

Ready Reference:

Day _____ Month _____ Day ___ Year _____

Spiritual: pray, praise, serve ...
Family: love, listen, laugh ...
Friends: reach out, encourage, share ...
Morning rituals: shower, dress, breakfast ...
Vitals: weight, blood pressure, etc.
Medical: medicines, treatments, etc.
Food & nutrition: morning, afternoon, evening (with calories) ...
Exercise: flexibility, cardio, resistance, sports ...
Financial:
Infrastructure: home, transportation,
Appointments:

To dos:	Accomplishments:

Calls to make:
Correspondence:
Delegated, postponed, declined:
Evening rituals: dinner, family, bed ...
Notes: search, look up, order ...

Journal:

Continuous Learning:

Day _____ Month _____ Day ___ Year _____

Day ____ Month _____ Day ___ Year _____

| Spiritual: pray, praise, serve … |
| Family: love, listen, laugh … |
| Friends: reach out, encourage, share … |
| Morning rituals: shower, dress, breakfast … |
| Vitals: weight, blood pressure, etc. |
| Medical: medicines, treatments, etc. |
| Food & nutrition: morning, afternoon, evening (with calories) … |
| Exercise: flexibility, cardio, resistance, sports … |
| Financial: |
| Infrastructure: home, transportation, |
| Appointments: |

To dos:	Accomplishments:

| Calls to make: |
| Correspondence: |
| Delegated, postponed, declined: |
| Evening rituals: dinner, family, bed … |
| Notes: search, look up, order … |

Journal:

Continuous Learning:

Day _____ Month _____ Day ___ Year _____

Day _____ Month _____ Day ____ Year _____

Spiritual: pray, praise, serve …	
Family: love, listen, laugh …	
Friends: reach out, encourage, share …	
Morning rituals: shower, dress, breakfast …	
Vitals: weight, blood pressure, etc.	
Medical: medicines, treatments, etc.	
Food & nutrition: morning, afternoon, evening (with calories) …	
Exercise: flexibility, cardio, resistance, sports …	
Financial:	
Infrastructure: home, transportation,	
Appointments:	

To dos:	Accomplishments:

Calls to make:
Correspondence:
Delegated, postponed, declined:
Evening rituals: dinner, family, bed …
Notes: search, look up, order …

Journal:

Continuous Learning:

Day _____ Month _____ Day ___ Year _____

Day _____ Month _____ Day ____ Year _____

| Spiritual: pray, praise, serve … |
| Family: love, listen, laugh … |
| Friends: reach out, encourage, share … |
| Morning rituals: shower, dress, breakfast … |
| Vitals: weight, blood pressure, etc. |
| Medical: medicines, treatments, etc. |
| Food & nutrition: morning, afternoon, evening (with calories) … |
| Exercise: flexibility, cardio, resistance, sports … |
| Financial: |
| Infrastructure: home, transportation, |
| Appointments: |

To dos:	Accomplishments:

Calls to make:

Correspondence:

Delegated, postponed, declined:

Evening rituals: dinner, family, bed …

Notes: search, look up, order …

Journal:

Continuous Learning:

Day _____ Month _____ Day ___ Year _____

Day _____ Month _____ Day ____ Year _____

| Spiritual: pray, praise, serve … |
| Family: love, listen, laugh … |
| Friends: reach out, encourage, share … |
| Morning rituals: shower, dress, breakfast … |
| Vitals: weight, blood pressure, etc. |
| Medical: medicines, treatments, etc. |
| Food & nutrition: morning, afternoon, evening (with calories) … |
| Exercise: flexibility, cardio, resistance, sports … |
| Financial: |
| Infrastructure: home, transportation, |
| Appointments: |

To dos:	Accomplishments:

| Calls to make: |
| Correspondence: |
| Delegated, postponed, declined: |
| Evening rituals: dinner, family, bed … |
| Notes: search, look up, order … |

Journal:

Continuous Learning:

Day _____ Month _____ Day ___ Year _____

Day ____ Month _____ Day ___ Year _____

| Spiritual: pray, praise, serve ... |
| Family: love, listen, laugh ... |
| Friends: reach out, encourage, share ... |
| Morning rituals: shower, dress, breakfast ... |
| Vitals: weight, blood pressure, etc. |
| Medical: medicines, treatments, etc. |
| Food & nutrition: morning, afternoon, evening (with calories) ... |
| Exercise: flexibility, cardio, resistance, sports ... |
| Financial: |
| Infrastructure: home, transportation, |
| Appointments: |

To dos:	Accomplishments:

| Calls to make: |
| Correspondence: |
| Delegated, postponed, declined: |
| Evening rituals: dinner, family, bed ... |
| Notes: search, look up, order ... |

Journal:

Continuous Learning:

Day _____ Month _____ Day ___ Year _____

Day _____ Month _____ Day ____ Year _____

| Spiritual: pray, praise, serve … |
| Family: love, listen, laugh … |
| Friends: reach out, encourage, share … |
| Morning rituals: shower, dress, breakfast … |
| Vitals: weight, blood pressure, etc. |
| Medical: medicines, treatments, etc. |
| Food & nutrition: morning, afternoon, evening (with calories) … |
| Exercise: flexibility, cardio, resistance, sports … |
| Financial: |
| Infrastructure: home, transportation, |
| Appointments: |

To dos:	Accomplishments:

| Calls to make: |
| Correspondence: |
| Delegated, postponed, declined: |
| Evening rituals: dinner, family, bed … |
| Notes: search, look up, order … |

| Journal: |
| |

| Continuous Learning: |

Day _____ Month _____ Day ___ Year _____

Day _____ Month _____ Day ___ Year _____

Spiritual: pray, praise, serve ...	
Family: love, listen, laugh ...	
Friends: reach out, encourage, share ...	
Morning rituals: shower, dress, breakfast ...	
Vitals: weight, blood pressure, etc.	
Medical: medicines, treatments, etc.	
Food & nutrition: morning, afternoon, evening (with calories) ...	
Exercise: flexibility, cardio, resistance, sports ...	
Financial:	
Infrastructure: home, transportation,	
Appointments:	

To dos:	Accomplishments:

Calls to make:
Correspondence:
Delegated, postponed, declined:
Evening rituals: dinner, family, bed ...
Notes: search, look up, order ...

Journal:

Continuous Learning:

Day _____ Month _____ Day ___ Year _____

Day ____ Month _____ Day ___ Year _____

Spiritual: pray, praise, serve …	
Family: love, listen, laugh …	
Friends: reach out, encourage, share …	
Morning rituals: shower, dress, breakfast …	
Vitals: weight, blood pressure, etc.	
Medical: medicines, treatments, etc.	
Food & nutrition: morning, afternoon, evening (with calories) …	
Exercise: flexibility, cardio, resistance, sports …	
Financial:	
Infrastructure: home, transportation,	
Appointments:	

To dos:	Accomplishments:

Calls to make:

Correspondence:

Delegated, postponed, declined:

Evening rituals: dinner, family, bed …

Notes: search, look up, order …

Journal:

Continuous Learning:

Day _____ Month _____ Day ___ Year _____

Day _____ Month _____ Day ___ Year _____

Spiritual: pray, praise, serve ...
Family: love, listen, laugh ...
Friends: reach out, encourage, share ...
Morning rituals: shower, dress, breakfast ...
Vitals: weight, blood pressure, etc.
Medical: medicines, treatments, etc.
Food & nutrition: morning, afternoon, evening (with calories) ...
Exercise: flexibility, cardio, resistance, sports ...
Financial:
Infrastructure: home, transportation,
Appointments:

To dos:	Accomplishments:

Calls to make:
Correspondence:
Delegated, postponed, declined:
Evening rituals: dinner, family, bed ...
Notes: search, look up, order ...
Journal:
Continuous Learning:

Day _____ Month _____ Day ___ Year _____

Day _____ Month _____ Day ____ Year _____

Spiritual: pray, praise, serve …	
Family: love, listen, laugh …	
Friends: reach out, encourage, share …	
Morning rituals: shower, dress, breakfast …	
Vitals: weight, blood pressure, etc.	
Medical: medicines, treatments, etc.	
Food & nutrition: morning, afternoon, evening (with calories) …	
Exercise: flexibility, cardio, resistance, sports …	
Financial:	
Infrastructure: home, transportation,	
Appointments:	

To dos:	Accomplishments:

Calls to make:

Correspondence:

Delegated, postponed, declined:

Evening rituals: dinner, family, bed …

Notes: search, look up, order …

Journal:

Continuous Learning:

Day _____ Month _____ Day ___ Year _____

Day _____ Month _____ Day ___ Year _____

Spiritual: pray, praise, serve …	
Family: love, listen, laugh …	
Friends: reach out, encourage, share …	
Morning rituals: shower, dress, breakfast …	
Vitals: weight, blood pressure, etc.	
Medical: medicines, treatments, etc.	
Food & nutrition: morning, afternoon, evening (with calories) …	
Exercise: flexibility, cardio, resistance, sports …	
Financial:	
Infrastructure: home, transportation,	
Appointments:	

To dos:	Accomplishments:

Calls to make:

Correspondence:

Delegated, postponed, declined:

Evening rituals: dinner, family, bed …

Notes: search, look up, order …

Journal:

Continuous Learning:

Day _____ Month _____ Day ___ Year _____

Day _____ Month _____ Day ___ Year _____

Spiritual: pray, praise, serve …	
Family: love, listen, laugh …	
Friends: reach out, encourage, share …	
Morning rituals: shower, dress, breakfast …	
Vitals: weight, blood pressure, etc.	
Medical: medicines, treatments, etc.	
Food & nutrition: morning, afternoon, evening (with calories) …	
Exercise: flexibility, cardio, resistance, sports …	
Financial:	
Infrastructure: home, transportation,	
Appointments:	

To dos:	Accomplishments:

Calls to make:

Correspondence:

Delegated, postponed, declined:

Evening rituals: dinner, family, bed …

Notes: search, look up, order …

Journal:

Continuous Learning:

Day _____ Month _____ Day ___ Year _____

| Spiritual: pray, praise, serve … |
| Family: love, listen, laugh … |
| Friends: reach out, encourage, share … |
| Morning rituals: shower, dress, breakfast … |
| Vitals: weight, blood pressure, etc. |
| Medical: medicines, treatments, etc. |
| Food & nutrition: morning, afternoon, evening (with calories) … |
| Exercise: flexibility, cardio, resistance, sports … |
| Financial: |
| Infrastructure: home, transportation, |
| Appointments: |

To dos:	Accomplishments:

| Calls to make: |
| Correspondence: |
| Delegated, postponed, declined: |
| Evening rituals: dinner, family, bed … |
| Notes: search, look up, order … |

Journal:

Continuous Learning:

Day _____ Month _____ Day ___ Year _____

Day _____ Month _____ Day ____ Year _____

| Spiritual: pray, praise, serve ... |
| Family: love, listen, laugh ... |
| Friends: reach out, encourage, share ... |
| Morning rituals: shower, dress, breakfast ... |
| Vitals: weight, blood pressure, etc. |
| Medical: medicines, treatments, etc. |
| Food & nutrition: morning, afternoon, evening (with calories) ... |
| Exercise: flexibility, cardio, resistance, sports ... |
| Financial: |
| Infrastructure: home, transportation, |
| Appointments: |

To dos:	Accomplishments:

| Calls to make: |
| Correspondence: |
| Delegated, postponed, declined: |
| Evening rituals: dinner, family, bed ... |
| Notes: search, look up, order ... |

Journal:

Continuous Learning:

Day _____ Month _____ Day ___ Year _____

Day _____ Month _____ Day ____ Year _____

Spiritual: pray, praise, serve …
Family: love, listen, laugh …
Friends: reach out, encourage, share …
Morning rituals: shower, dress, breakfast …
Vitals: weight, blood pressure, etc.
Medical: medicines, treatments, etc.
Food & nutrition: morning, afternoon, evening (with calories) …
Exercise: flexibility, cardio, resistance, sports …
Financial:
Infrastructure: home, transportation,
Appointments:

To dos:	Accomplishments:

Calls to make:
Correspondence:
Delegated, postponed, declined:
Evening rituals: dinner, family, bed …
Notes: search, look up, order …

Journal:

Continuous Learning:

Day _____ Month _____ Day ___ Year _____

Day _____ Month _____ Day ___ Year _____

Spiritual: pray, praise, serve ...	
Family: love, listen, laugh ...	
Friends: reach out, encourage, share ...	
Morning rituals: shower, dress, breakfast ...	
Vitals: weight, blood pressure, etc.	
Medical: medicines, treatments, etc.	
Food & nutrition: morning, afternoon, evening (with calories) ...	
Exercise: flexibility, cardio, resistance, sports ...	
Financial:	
Infrastructure: home, transportation,	
Appointments:	

To dos:	Accomplishments:

Calls to make:

Correspondence:

Delegated, postponed, declined:

Evening rituals: dinner, family, bed ...

Notes: search, look up, order ...

Journal:

Continuous Learning:

Day _____ Month _____ Day ___ Year _____

Day _____ Month _____ Day ___ Year _____

Spiritual: pray, praise, serve …
Family: love, listen, laugh …
Friends: reach out, encourage, share …
Morning rituals: shower, dress, breakfast …
Vitals: weight, blood pressure, etc.
Medical: medicines, treatments, etc.
Food & nutrition: morning, afternoon, evening (with calories) …
Exercise: flexibility, cardio, resistance, sports …
Financial:
Infrastructure: home, transportation,
Appointments:

To dos:	Accomplishments:

Calls to make:
Correspondence:
Delegated, postponed, declined:
Evening rituals: dinner, family, bed …
Notes: search, look up, order …

Journal:

Continuous Learning:

Day _____ Month _____ Day ___ Year _____

Day ____ Month _____ Day ___ Year _____

| Spiritual: pray, praise, serve … |
| Family: love, listen, laugh … |
| Friends: reach out, encourage, share … |
| Morning rituals: shower, dress, breakfast … |
| Vitals: weight, blood pressure, etc. |
| Medical: medicines, treatments, etc. |
| Food & nutrition: morning, afternoon, evening (with calories) … |
| Exercise: flexibility, cardio, resistance, sports … |
| Financial: |
| Infrastructure: home, transportation, |
| Appointments: |

To dos:	Accomplishments:

| Calls to make: |
| Correspondence: |
| Delegated, postponed, declined: |
| Evening rituals: dinner, family, bed … |
| Notes: search, look up, order … |

| Journal: |

| Continuous Learning: |

Day _____ Month _____ Day ___ Year _____

Day _____ Month _____ Day ____ Year _____

Spiritual: pray, praise, serve …	
Family: love, listen, laugh …	
Friends: reach out, encourage, share …	
Morning rituals: shower, dress, breakfast …	
Vitals: weight, blood pressure, etc.	
Medical: medicines, treatments, etc.	
Food & nutrition: morning, afternoon, evening (with calories) …	
Exercise: flexibility, cardio, resistance, sports …	
Financial:	
Infrastructure: home, transportation,	
Appointments:	

To dos:	Accomplishments:

Calls to make:
Correspondence:
Delegated, postponed, declined:
Evening rituals: dinner, family, bed …
Notes: search, look up, order …
Journal:
Continuous Learning:

Day _____ Month _____ Day ___ Year _____

Day _____ Month _____ Day ____ Year _____

| Spiritual: pray, praise, serve … |
| Family: love, listen, laugh … |
| Friends: reach out, encourage, share … |
| Morning rituals: shower, dress, breakfast … |
| Vitals: weight, blood pressure, etc. |
| Medical: medicines, treatments, etc. |
| Food & nutrition: morning, afternoon, evening (with calories) … |
| Exercise: flexibility, cardio, resistance, sports … |
| Financial: |
| Infrastructure: home, transportation, |
| Appointments: |

To dos:	Accomplishments:

| Calls to make: |
| Correspondence: |
| Delegated, postponed, declined: |
| Evening rituals: dinner, family, bed … |
| Notes: search, look up, order … |

Journal:

Continuous Learning:

Day _____ Month _____ Day ___ Year _____

Day ____ Month _____ Day ___ Year _____

Spiritual: pray, praise, serve ...
Family: love, listen, laugh ...
Friends: reach out, encourage, share ...
Morning rituals: shower, dress, breakfast ...
Vitals: weight, blood pressure, etc.
Medical: medicines, treatments, etc.
Food & nutrition: morning, afternoon, evening (with calories) ...
Exercise: flexibility, cardio, resistance, sports ...
Financial:
Infrastructure: home, transportation,
Appointments:

To dos:	Accomplishments:

Calls to make:
Correspondence:
Delegated, postponed, declined:
Evening rituals: dinner, family, bed ...
Notes: search, look up, order ...

Journal:

Continuous Learning:

Day _____ Month _____ Day ___ Year _____

Day _____ Month _____ Day ____ Year _____

Spiritual: pray, praise, serve …	
Family: love, listen, laugh …	
Friends: reach out, encourage, share …	
Morning rituals: shower, dress, breakfast …	
Vitals: weight, blood pressure, etc.	
Medical: medicines, treatments, etc.	
Food & nutrition: morning, afternoon, evening (with calories) …	
Exercise: flexibility, cardio, resistance, sports …	
Financial:	
Infrastructure: home, transportation,	
Appointments:	

To dos:	Accomplishments:

Calls to make:
Correspondence:
Delegated, postponed, declined:
Evening rituals: dinner, family, bed …
Notes: search, look up, order …
Journal:
Continuous Learning:

Day _____ Month _____ Day ___ Year _____

Day ____ Month _____ Day ___ Year _____

| Spiritual: pray, praise, serve ... |
| Family: love, listen, laugh ... |
| Friends: reach out, encourage, share ... |
| Morning rituals: shower, dress, breakfast ... |
| Vitals: weight, blood pressure, etc. |
| Medical: medicines, treatments, etc. |
| Food & nutrition: morning, afternoon, evening (with calories) ... |
| Exercise: flexibility, cardio, resistance, sports ... |
| Financial: |
| Infrastructure: home, transportation, |
| Appointments: |

To dos:	Accomplishments:

| Calls to make: |
| Correspondence: |
| Delegated, postponed, declined: |
| Evening rituals: dinner, family, bed ... |
| Notes: search, look up, order ... |

Journal:

Continuous Learning:

Day _____ Month _____ Day ___ Year _____

Day ____ Month _____ Day ___ Year _____

Spiritual: pray, praise, serve …	
Family: love, listen, laugh …	
Friends: reach out, encourage, share …	
Morning rituals: shower, dress, breakfast …	
Vitals: weight, blood pressure, etc.	
Medical: medicines, treatments, etc.	
Food & nutrition: morning, afternoon, evening (with calories) …	
Exercise: flexibility, cardio, resistance, sports …	
Financial:	
Infrastructure: home, transportation,	
Appointments:	

To dos:	Accomplishments:

Calls to make:

Correspondence:

Delegated, postponed, declined:

Evening rituals: dinner, family, bed …

Notes: search, look up, order …

Journal:

Continuous Learning:

Day _____ Month _____ Day ___ Year _____

Day _____ Month _____ Day ___ Year _____

Spiritual: pray, praise, serve ...
Family: love, listen, laugh ...
Friends: reach out, encourage, share ...
Morning rituals: shower, dress, breakfast ...
Vitals: weight, blood pressure, etc.
Medical: medicines, treatments, etc.
Food & nutrition: morning, afternoon, evening (with calories) ...
Exercise: flexibility, cardio, resistance, sports ...
Financial:
Infrastructure: home, transportation,
Appointments:

To dos:	Accomplishments:

Calls to make:
Correspondence:
Delegated, postponed, declined:
Evening rituals: dinner, family, bed ...
Notes: search, look up, order ...

Journal:

Continuous Learning:

Day _____ Month _____ Day ____ Year _____

Day _____ Month _____ Day ____ Year _____

| Spiritual: pray, praise, serve … |
| Family: love, listen, laugh … |
| Friends: reach out, encourage, share … |
| Morning rituals: shower, dress, breakfast … |
| Vitals: weight, blood pressure, etc. |
| Medical: medicines, treatments, etc. |
| Food & nutrition: morning, afternoon, evening (with calories) … |
| Exercise: flexibility, cardio, resistance, sports … |
| Financial: |
| Infrastructure: home, transportation, |
| Appointments: |

To dos:	Accomplishments:

| Calls to make: |
| Correspondence: |
| Delegated, postponed, declined: |
| Evening rituals: dinner, family, bed … |
| Notes: search, look up, order … |

Journal:

Continuous Learning:

Day _____ Month _____ Day ___ Year _____

Day _____ Month _____ Day ___ Year _____

| Spiritual: pray, praise, serve … |
| Family: love, listen, laugh … |
| Friends: reach out, encourage, share … |
| Morning rituals: shower, dress, breakfast … |
| Vitals: weight, blood pressure, etc. |
| Medical: medicines, treatments, etc. |
| Food & nutrition: morning, afternoon, evening (with calories) … |
| Exercise: flexibility, cardio, resistance, sports … |
| Financial: |
| Infrastructure: home, transportation, |
| Appointments: |

To dos:	Accomplishments:

| Calls to make: |
| Correspondence: |
| Delegated, postponed, declined: |
| Evening rituals: dinner, family, bed … |
| Notes: search, look up, order … |

Journal:

Continuous Learning:

Day _____ Month _____ Day ___ Year _____

Spiritual: pray, praise, serve …
Family: love, listen, laugh …
Friends: reach out, encourage, share …
Morning rituals: shower, dress, breakfast …
Vitals: weight, blood pressure, etc.
Medical: medicines, treatments, etc.
Food & nutrition: morning, afternoon, evening (with calories) …
Exercise: flexibility, cardio, resistance, sports …
Financial:
Infrastructure: home, transportation,
Appointments:

To dos:	Accomplishments:

Calls to make:
Correspondence:
Delegated, postponed, declined:
Evening rituals: dinner, family, bed …
Notes: search, look up, order …

Journal:

Continuous Learning:

Day _____ Month _____ Day ___ Year _____

Day _____ Month _____ Day ____ Year _____

Spiritual: pray, praise, serve …

Family: love, listen, laugh …

Friends: reach out, encourage, share …

Morning rituals: shower, dress, breakfast …

Vitals: weight, blood pressure, etc.

Medical: medicines, treatments, etc.

Food & nutrition: morning, afternoon, evening (with calories) …

Exercise: flexibility, cardio, resistance, sports …

Financial:

Infrastructure: home, transportation,

Appointments:

To dos:	Accomplishments:

Calls to make:

Correspondence:

Delegated, postponed, declined:

Evening rituals: dinner, family, bed …

Notes: search, look up, order …

Journal:

Continuous Learning:

Day _____ Month _____ Day ___ Year _____

Day _____ Month _____ Day ___ Year _____

Spiritual: pray, praise, serve …
Family: love, listen, laugh …
Friends: reach out, encourage, share …
Morning rituals: shower, dress, breakfast …
Vitals: weight, blood pressure, etc.
Medical: medicines, treatments, etc.
Food & nutrition: morning, afternoon, evening (with calories) …
Exercise: flexibility, cardio, resistance, sports …
Financial:
Infrastructure: home, transportation,
Appointments:

To dos:	Accomplishments:

Calls to make:
Correspondence:
Delegated, postponed, declined:
Evening rituals: dinner, family, bed …
Notes: search, look up, order …

Journal:

Continuous Learning:

Day _____ Month _____ Day ___ Year _____

Day _____ Month _____ Day ___ Year _____

Spiritual: pray, praise, serve ...
Family: love, listen, laugh ...
Friends: reach out, encourage, share ...
Morning rituals: shower, dress, breakfast ...
Vitals: weight, blood pressure, etc.
Medical: medicines, treatments, etc.
Food & nutrition: morning, afternoon, evening (with calories) ...
Exercise: flexibility, cardio, resistance, sports ...
Financial:
Infrastructure: home, transportation,
Appointments:

To dos:	Accomplishments:

Calls to make:
Correspondence:
Delegated, postponed, declined:
Evening rituals: dinner, family, bed ...
Notes: search, look up, order ...
Journal:
Continuous Learning:

Day _____ Month _____ Day _____ Year _____

| Spiritual: pray, praise, serve … |
| Family: love, listen, laugh … |
| Friends: reach out, encourage, share … |
| Morning rituals: shower, dress, breakfast … |
| Vitals: weight, blood pressure, etc. |
| Medical: medicines, treatments, etc. |
| Food & nutrition: morning, afternoon, evening (with calories) … |
| Exercise: flexibility, cardio, resistance, sports … |
| Financial: |
| Infrastructure: home, transportation, |
| Appointments: |

To dos:	Accomplishments:

| Calls to make: |
| Correspondence: |
| Delegated, postponed, declined: |
| Evening rituals: dinner, family, bed … |
| Notes: search, look up, order … |

Journal:

Continuous Learning:

Day _____ Month _____ Day ___ Year _____

Day _____ Month _____ Day ___ Year _____

Spiritual: pray, praise, serve ...	
Family: love, listen, laugh ...	
Friends: reach out, encourage, share ...	
Morning rituals: shower, dress, breakfast ...	
Vitals: weight, blood pressure, etc.	
Medical: medicines, treatments, etc.	
Food & nutrition: morning, afternoon, evening (with calories) ...	
Exercise: flexibility, cardio, resistance, sports ...	
Financial:	
Infrastructure: home, transportation,	
Appointments:	

To dos:	Accomplishments:

Calls to make:

Correspondence:

Delegated, postponed, declined:

Evening rituals: dinner, family, bed ...

Notes: search, look up, order ...

Journal:

Continuous Learning:

Day _____ Month _____ Day ___ Year _____

Day ____ Month _____ Day ___ Year _____

Spiritual: pray, praise, serve …	
Family: love, listen, laugh …	
Friends: reach out, encourage, share …	
Morning rituals: shower, dress, breakfast …	
Vitals: weight, blood pressure, etc.	
Medical: medicines, treatments, etc.	
Food & nutrition: morning, afternoon, evening (with calories) …	
Exercise: flexibility, cardio, resistance, sports …	
Financial:	
Infrastructure: home, transportation,	
Appointments:	

To dos:	Accomplishments:

Calls to make:

Correspondence:

Delegated, postponed, declined:

Evening rituals: dinner, family, bed …

Notes: search, look up, order …

Journal:

Continuous Learning:

Day _____ Month _____ Day ___ Year _____

Day _____ Month _____ Day ___ Year _____

Spiritual: pray, praise, serve ...	
Family: love, listen, laugh ...	
Friends: reach out, encourage, share ...	
Morning rituals: shower, dress, breakfast ...	
Vitals: weight, blood pressure, etc.	
Medical: medicines, treatments, etc.	
Food & nutrition: morning, afternoon, evening (with calories) ...	
Exercise: flexibility, cardio, resistance, sports ...	
Financial:	
Infrastructure: home, transportation,	
Appointments:	

To dos:	Accomplishments:

Calls to make:

Correspondence:

Delegated, postponed, declined:

Evening rituals: dinner, family, bed ...

Notes: search, look up, order ...

Journal:

Continuous Learning:

Day _____ Month _____ Day ___ Year _____

Day _____ Month _____ Day ____ Year _____

| Spiritual: pray, praise, serve … |
| Family: love, listen, laugh … |
| Friends: reach out, encourage, share … |
| Morning rituals: shower, dress, breakfast … |
| Vitals: weight, blood pressure, etc. |
| Medical: medicines, treatments, etc. |
| Food & nutrition: morning, afternoon, evening (with calories) … |
| Exercise: flexibility, cardio, resistance, sports … |
| Financial: |
| Infrastructure: home, transportation, |
| Appointments: |

To dos:	Accomplishments:

| Calls to make: |
| Correspondence: |
| Delegated, postponed, declined: |
| Evening rituals: dinner, family, bed … |
| Notes: search, look up, order … |

Journal:

Continuous Learning:

Day _____ Month _____ Day ___ Year _____

Day _____ Month _____ Day ____ Year _____

Spiritual: pray, praise, serve …
Family: love, listen, laugh …
Friends: reach out, encourage, share …
Morning rituals: shower, dress, breakfast …
Vitals: weight, blood pressure, etc.
Medical: medicines, treatments, etc.
Food & nutrition: morning, afternoon, evening (with calories) …
Exercise: flexibility, cardio, resistance, sports …
Financial:
Infrastructure: home, transportation,
Appointments:

To dos:	Accomplishments:

Calls to make:
Correspondence:
Delegated, postponed, declined:
Evening rituals: dinner, family, bed …
Notes: search, look up, order …
Journal:
Continuous Learning:

Day _____ Month _____ Day ___ Year _____

Day _____ Month _____ Day ____ Year _____

| Spiritual: pray, praise, serve … |
| Family: love, listen, laugh … |
| Friends: reach out, encourage, share … |
| Morning rituals: shower, dress, breakfast … |
| Vitals: weight, blood pressure, etc. |
| Medical: medicines, treatments, etc. |
| Food & nutrition: morning, afternoon, evening (with calories) … |
| Exercise: flexibility, cardio, resistance, sports … |
| Financial: |
| Infrastructure: home, transportation, |
| Appointments: |

To dos:	Accomplishments:

| Calls to make: |
| Correspondence: |
| Delegated, postponed, declined: |
| Evening rituals: dinner, family, bed … |
| Notes: search, look up, order … |
| Journal: |
| Continuous Learning: |

Day _____ Month _____ Day ___ Year _____

Day ____ Month _____ Day ___ Year _____

| Spiritual: pray, praise, serve … |
| Family: love, listen, laugh … |
| Friends: reach out, encourage, share … |
| Morning rituals: shower, dress, breakfast … |
| Vitals: weight, blood pressure, etc. |
| Medical: medicines, treatments, etc. |
| Food & nutrition: morning, afternoon, evening (with calories) … |
| Exercise: flexibility, cardio, resistance, sports … |
| Financial: |
| Infrastructure: home, transportation, |
| Appointments: |

To dos:	Accomplishments:

| Calls to make: |
| Correspondence: |
| Delegated, postponed, declined: |
| Evening rituals: dinner, family, bed … |
| Notes: search, look up, order … |

| Journal: |

| Continuous Learning: |

Day _____ Month _____ Day ___ Year _____

Day _____ Month _____ Day ___ Year _____

Spiritual: pray, praise, serve ...	
Family: love, listen, laugh ...	
Friends: reach out, encourage, share ...	
Morning rituals: shower, dress, breakfast ...	
Vitals: weight, blood pressure, etc.	
Medical: medicines, treatments, etc.	
Food & nutrition: morning, afternoon, evening (with calories) ...	
Exercise: flexibility, cardio, resistance, sports ...	
Financial:	
Infrastructure: home, transportation,	
Appointments:	

To dos:	Accomplishments:

Calls to make:

Correspondence:

Delegated, postponed, declined:

Evening rituals: dinner, family, bed ...

Notes: search, look up, order ...

Journal:

Continuous Learning:

Day _____ Month _____ Day ___ Year _____

Day _____ Month _____ Day ____ Year _____

| Spiritual: pray, praise, serve ... |
| Family: love, listen, laugh ... |
| Friends: reach out, encourage, share ... |
| Morning rituals: shower, dress, breakfast ... |
| Vitals: weight, blood pressure, etc. |
| Medical: medicines, treatments, etc. |
| Food & nutrition: morning, afternoon, evening (with calories) ... |
| Exercise: flexibility, cardio, resistance, sports ... |
| Financial: |
| Infrastructure: home, transportation, |
| Appointments: |

To dos:	Accomplishments:

| Calls to make: |
| Correspondence: |
| Delegated, postponed, declined: |
| Evening rituals: dinner, family, bed ... |
| Notes: search, look up, order ... |

| Journal: |

| Continuous Learning: |

Day ____ Month _____ Day ___ Year _____

Spiritual: pray, praise, serve …	
Family: love, listen, laugh …	
Friends: reach out, encourage, share …	
Morning rituals: shower, dress, breakfast …	
Vitals: weight, blood pressure, etc.	
Medical: medicines, treatments, etc.	
Food & nutrition: morning, afternoon, evening (with calories) …	
Exercise: flexibility, cardio, resistance, sports …	
Financial:	
Infrastructure: home, transportation,	
Appointments:	

To dos:	Accomplishments:

Calls to make:

Correspondence:

Delegated, postponed, declined:

Evening rituals: dinner, family, bed …

Notes: search, look up, order …

Journal:

Continuous Learning:

Day _____ Month _____ Day ___ Year _____

Day ____ Month _____ Day ___ Year _____

Spiritual: pray, praise, serve ...

Family: love, listen, laugh ...

Friends: reach out, encourage, share ...

Morning rituals: shower, dress, breakfast ...

Vitals: weight, blood pressure, etc.

Medical: medicines, treatments, etc.

Food & nutrition: morning, afternoon, evening (with calories) ...

Exercise: flexibility, cardio, resistance, sports ...

Financial:

Infrastructure: home, transportation,

Appointments:

To dos:	Accomplishments:

Calls to make:

Correspondence:

Delegated, postponed, declined:

Evening rituals: dinner, family, bed ...

Notes: search, look up, order ...

Journal:

Continuous Learning:

Day _____ Month _____ Day ___ Year _____

Day _____ Month _____ Day ____ Year _____

| Spiritual: pray, praise, serve … |
| Family: love, listen, laugh … |
| Friends: reach out, encourage, share … |
| Morning rituals: shower, dress, breakfast … |
| Vitals: weight, blood pressure, etc. |
| Medical: medicines, treatments, etc. |
| Food & nutrition: morning, afternoon, evening (with calories) … |
| Exercise: flexibility, cardio, resistance, sports … |
| Financial: |
| Infrastructure: home, transportation, |
| Appointments: |

To dos:	Accomplishments:

| Calls to make: |
| Correspondence: |
| Delegated, postponed, declined: |
| Evening rituals: dinner, family, bed … |
| Notes: search, look up, order … |

Journal:

Continuous Learning:

Day _____ Month _____ Day ___ Year _____

Day _____ Month _____ Day _____ Year _____

| Spiritual: pray, praise, serve … |
| Family: love, listen, laugh … |
| Friends: reach out, encourage, share … |
| Morning rituals: shower, dress, breakfast … |
| Vitals: weight, blood pressure, etc. |
| Medical: medicines, treatments, etc. |
| Food & nutrition: morning, afternoon, evening (with calories) … |
| Exercise: flexibility, cardio, resistance, sports … |
| Financial: |
| Infrastructure: home, transportation, |
| Appointments: |

To dos:	Accomplishments:

| Calls to make: |
| Correspondence: |
| Delegated, postponed, declined: |
| Evening rituals: dinner, family, bed … |
| Notes: search, look up, order … |

| Journal: |

| Continuous Learning: |

Day _____ Month _____ Day ___ Year _____

Day ____ Month _____ Day ___ Year _____

Spiritual: pray, praise, serve …
Family: love, listen, laugh …
Friends: reach out, encourage, share …
Morning rituals: shower, dress, breakfast …
Vitals: weight, blood pressure, etc.
Medical: medicines, treatments, etc.
Food & nutrition: morning, afternoon, evening (with calories) …
Exercise: flexibility, cardio, resistance, sports …
Financial:
Infrastructure: home, transportation,
Appointments:

To dos:	Accomplishments:

Calls to make:
Correspondence:
Delegated, postponed, declined:
Evening rituals: dinner, family, bed …
Notes: search, look up, order …
Journal:
Continuous Learning:

Day ____ Month _____ Day ___ Year _____

| Spiritual: pray, praise, serve ... |
| Family: love, listen, laugh ... |
| Friends: reach out, encourage, share ... |
| Morning rituals: shower, dress, breakfast ... |
| Vitals: weight, blood pressure, etc. |
| Medical: medicines, treatments, etc. |
| Food & nutrition: morning, afternoon, evening (with calories) ... |
| Exercise: flexibility, cardio, resistance, sports ... |
| Financial: |
| Infrastructure: home, transportation, |
| Appointments: |

To dos:	Accomplishments:

| Calls to make: |
| Correspondence: |
| Delegated, postponed, declined: |
| Evening rituals: dinner, family, bed ... |
| Notes: search, look up, order ... |

Journal:

Continuous Learning:

Day _____ Month _____ Day ___ Year _____

Spiritual: pray, praise, serve ...	
Family: love, listen, laugh ...	
Friends: reach out, encourage, share ...	
Morning rituals: shower, dress, breakfast ...	
Vitals: weight, blood pressure, etc.	
Medical: medicines, treatments, etc.	
Food & nutrition: morning, afternoon, evening (with calories) ...	
Exercise: flexibility, cardio, resistance, sports ...	
Financial:	
Infrastructure: home, transportation,	
Appointments:	

To dos:	Accomplishments:

Calls to make:
Correspondence:
Delegated, postponed, declined:
Evening rituals: dinner, family, bed ...
Notes: search, look up, order ...
Journal:
Continuous Learning:

Day _____ Month _____ Day ___ Year _____

Day _____ Month _____ Day _____ Year _____

Spiritual: pray, praise, serve …	
Family: love, listen, laugh …	
Friends: reach out, encourage, share …	
Morning rituals: shower, dress, breakfast …	
Vitals: weight, blood pressure, etc.	
Medical: medicines, treatments, etc.	
Food & nutrition: morning, afternoon, evening (with calories) …	
Exercise: flexibility, cardio, resistance, sports …	
Financial:	
Infrastructure: home, transportation,	
Appointments:	

To dos:	Accomplishments:

Calls to make:

Correspondence:

Delegated, postponed, declined:

Evening rituals: dinner, family, bed …

Notes: search, look up, order …

Journal:

Continuous Learning:

Day _____ Month _____ Day ___ Year _____

Day _____ Month _____ Day ___ Year _____

Spiritual: pray, praise, serve ...	
Family: love, listen, laugh ...	
Friends: reach out, encourage, share ...	
Morning rituals: shower, dress, breakfast ...	
Vitals: weight, blood pressure, etc.	
Medical: medicines, treatments, etc.	
Food & nutrition: morning, afternoon, evening (with calories) ...	
Exercise: flexibility, cardio, resistance, sports ...	
Financial:	
Infrastructure: home, transportation,	
Appointments:	

To dos:	Accomplishments:

Calls to make:

Correspondence:

Delegated, postponed, declined:

Evening rituals: dinner, family, bed ...

Notes: search, look up, order ...

Journal:

Continuous Learning:

Day _____ Month _____ Day ___ Year _____

Day _____ Month _____ Day ____ Year _____

| Spiritual: pray, praise, serve … |
| Family: love, listen, laugh … |
| Friends: reach out, encourage, share … |
| Morning rituals: shower, dress, breakfast … |
| Vitals: weight, blood pressure, etc. |
| Medical: medicines, treatments, etc. |
| Food & nutrition: morning, afternoon, evening (with calories) … |
| Exercise: flexibility, cardio, resistance, sports … |
| Financial: |
| Infrastructure: home, transportation, |
| Appointments: |

To dos:	Accomplishments:

| Calls to make: |
| Correspondence: |
| Delegated, postponed, declined: |
| Evening rituals: dinner, family, bed … |
| Notes: search, look up, order … |

Journal:

Continuous Learning:

Day _____ Month _____ Day ___ Year _____

Day ____ Month _____ Day ___ Year _____

| Spiritual: pray, praise, serve ... |
| Family: love, listen, laugh ... |
| Friends: reach out, encourage, share ... |
| Morning rituals: shower, dress, breakfast ... |
| Vitals: weight, blood pressure, etc. |
| Medical: medicines, treatments, etc. |
| Food & nutrition: morning, afternoon, evening (with calories) ... |
| Exercise: flexibility, cardio, resistance, sports ... |
| Financial: |
| Infrastructure: home, transportation, |
| Appointments: |

To dos:	Accomplishments:

| Calls to make: |
| Correspondence: |
| Delegated, postponed, declined: |
| Evening rituals: dinner, family, bed ... |
| Notes: search, look up, order ... |

Journal:

Continuous Learning:

Day _____ Month _____ Day ___ Year _____

Day _____ Month _____ Day ____ Year _____

| Spiritual: pray, praise, serve ... |
| Family: love, listen, laugh ... |
| Friends: reach out, encourage, share ... |
| Morning rituals: shower, dress, breakfast ... |
| Vitals: weight, blood pressure, etc. |
| Medical: medicines, treatments, etc. |
| Food & nutrition: morning, afternoon, evening (with calories) ... |
| Exercise: flexibility, cardio, resistance, sports ... |
| Financial: |
| Infrastructure: home, transportation, |
| Appointments: |

To dos:	Accomplishments:

| Calls to make: |
| Correspondence: |
| Delegated, postponed, declined: |
| Evening rituals: dinner, family, bed ... |
| Notes: search, look up, order ... |

Journal:

Continuous Learning:

Day _____ Month _____ Day ___ Year _____

Day ____ Month _____ Day ___ Year _____

| Spiritual: pray, praise, serve ... |
| Family: love, listen, laugh ... |
| Friends: reach out, encourage, share ... |
| Morning rituals: shower, dress, breakfast ... |
| Vitals: weight, blood pressure, etc. |
| Medical: medicines, treatments, etc. |
| Food & nutrition: morning, afternoon, evening (with calories) ... |
| Exercise: flexibility, cardio, resistance, sports ... |
| Financial: |
| Infrastructure: home, transportation, |
| Appointments: |

To dos:	Accomplishments:

| Calls to make: |
| Correspondence: |
| Delegated, postponed, declined: |
| Evening rituals: dinner, family, bed ... |
| Notes: search, look up, order ... |

Journal:

Continuous Learning:

Day _____ Month _____ Day ___ Year _____

Day _____ Month _____ Day ____ Year _____

Spiritual: pray, praise, serve …	
Family: love, listen, laugh …	
Friends: reach out, encourage, share …	
Morning rituals: shower, dress, breakfast …	
Vitals: weight, blood pressure, etc.	
Medical: medicines, treatments, etc.	
Food & nutrition: morning, afternoon, evening (with calories) …	
Exercise: flexibility, cardio, resistance, sports …	
Financial:	
Infrastructure: home, transportation,	
Appointments:	

To dos:	Accomplishments:

Calls to make:

Correspondence:

Delegated, postponed, declined:

Evening rituals: dinner, family, bed …

Notes: search, look up, order …

Journal:

Continuous Learning:

Day _____ Month _____ Day ___ Year _____

Day ____ Month _____ Day ___ Year _____

Spiritual: pray, praise, serve ...	
Family: love, listen, laugh ...	
Friends: reach out, encourage, share ...	
Morning rituals: shower, dress, breakfast ...	
Vitals: weight, blood pressure, etc.	
Medical: medicines, treatments, etc.	
Food & nutrition: morning, afternoon, evening (with calories) ...	
Exercise: flexibility, cardio, resistance, sports ...	
Financial:	
Infrastructure: home, transportation,	
Appointments:	

To dos:	Accomplishments:

Calls to make:

Correspondence:

Delegated, postponed, declined:

Evening rituals: dinner, family, bed ...

Notes: search, look up, order ...

Journal:

Continuous Learning:

Day _____ Month _____ Day ___ Year _____

Day _____ Month _____ Day ____ Year _____

Spiritual: pray, praise, serve …
Family: love, listen, laugh …
Friends: reach out, encourage, share …
Morning rituals: shower, dress, breakfast …
Vitals: weight, blood pressure, etc.
Medical: medicines, treatments, etc.
Food & nutrition: morning, afternoon, evening (with calories) …
Exercise: flexibility, cardio, resistance, sports …
Financial:
Infrastructure: home, transportation,
Appointments:

To dos:	Accomplishments:

Calls to make:
Correspondence:
Delegated, postponed, declined:
Evening rituals: dinner, family, bed …
Notes: search, look up, order …

Journal:

Continuous Learning:

Day _____ Month _____ Day ____ Year _____

Day ____ Month _____ Day ___ Year _____

Spiritual: pray, praise, serve ...	
Family: love, listen, laugh ...	
Friends: reach out, encourage, share ...	
Morning rituals: shower, dress, breakfast ...	
Vitals: weight, blood pressure, etc.	
Medical: medicines, treatments, etc.	
Food & nutrition: morning, afternoon, evening (with calories) ...	
Exercise: flexibility, cardio, resistance, sports ...	
Financial:	
Infrastructure: home, transportation,	
Appointments:	

To dos:	Accomplishments:

Calls to make:

Correspondence:

Delegated, postponed, declined:

Evening rituals: dinner, family, bed ...

Notes: search, look up, order ...

Journal:

Continuous Learning:

Day _____ Month _____ Day ___ Year _____

Spiritual: pray, praise, serve …
Family: love, listen, laugh …
Friends: reach out, encourage, share …
Morning rituals: shower, dress, breakfast …
Vitals: weight, blood pressure, etc.
Medical: medicines, treatments, etc.
Food & nutrition: morning, afternoon, evening (with calories) …
Exercise: flexibility, cardio, resistance, sports …
Financial:
Infrastructure: home, transportation,
Appointments:

To dos:	Accomplishments:

Calls to make:
Correspondence:
Delegated, postponed, declined:
Evening rituals: dinner, family, bed …
Notes: search, look up, order …

Journal:

Continuous Learning:

Day _____ Month _____ Day ___ Year _____

Day ____ Month _____ Day ___ Year _____

Spiritual: pray, praise, serve …	
Family: love, listen, laugh …	
Friends: reach out, encourage, share …	
Morning rituals: shower, dress, breakfast …	
Vitals: weight, blood pressure, etc.	
Medical: medicines, treatments, etc.	
Food & nutrition: morning, afternoon, evening (with calories) …	
Exercise: flexibility, cardio, resistance, sports …	
Financial:	
Infrastructure: home, transportation,	
Appointments:	

To dos:	Accomplishments:

Calls to make:

Correspondence:

Delegated, postponed, declined:

Evening rituals: dinner, family, bed …

Notes: search, look up, order …

Journal:

Continuous Learning:

Day ____ Month _____ Day ___ Year _____

| Spiritual: pray, praise, serve … |
| Family: love, listen, laugh … |
| Friends: reach out, encourage, share … |
| Morning rituals: shower, dress, breakfast … |
| Vitals: weight, blood pressure, etc. |
| Medical: medicines, treatments, etc. |
| Food & nutrition: morning, afternoon, evening (with calories) … |
| Exercise: flexibility, cardio, resistance, sports … |
| Financial: |
| Infrastructure: home, transportation, |
| Appointments: |

To dos:	Accomplishments:

| Calls to make: |
| Correspondence: |
| Delegated, postponed, declined: |
| Evening rituals: dinner, family, bed … |
| Notes: search, look up, order … |

Journal:

Continuous Learning:

Day _____ Month _____ Day ____ Year _____

Day ____ Month _____ Day ___ Year _____

| Spiritual: pray, praise, serve … |
| Family: love, listen, laugh … |
| Friends: reach out, encourage, share … |
| Morning rituals: shower, dress, breakfast … |
| Vitals: weight, blood pressure, etc. |
| Medical: medicines, treatments, etc. |
| Food & nutrition: morning, afternoon, evening (with calories) … |
| Exercise: flexibility, cardio, resistance, sports … |
| Financial: |
| Infrastructure: home, transportation, |
| Appointments: |

To dos:	Accomplishments:

| Calls to make: |
| Correspondence: |
| Delegated, postponed, declined: |
| Evening rituals: dinner, family, bed … |
| Notes: search, look up, order … |

Journal:

Continuous Learning:

Day _____ Month _____ Day ___ Year _____

Day _____ Month _____ Day ____ Year _____

| Spiritual: pray, praise, serve … |
| Family: love, listen, laugh … |
| Friends: reach out, encourage, share … |
| Morning rituals: shower, dress, breakfast … |
| Vitals: weight, blood pressure, etc. |
| Medical: medicines, treatments, etc. |
| Food & nutrition: morning, afternoon, evening (with calories) … |
| Exercise: flexibility, cardio, resistance, sports … |
| Financial: |
| Infrastructure: home, transportation, |
| Appointments: |

To dos:	Accomplishments:

| Calls to make: |
| Correspondence: |
| Delegated, postponed, declined: |
| Evening rituals: dinner, family, bed … |
| Notes: search, look up, order … |

Journal:

Continuous Learning:

Day _____ Month _____ Day ___ Year _____

Day ____ Month _____ Day ___ Year _____

| Spiritual: pray, praise, serve … |
| Family: love, listen, laugh … |
| Friends: reach out, encourage, share … |
| Morning rituals: shower, dress, breakfast … |
| Vitals: weight, blood pressure, etc. |
| Medical: medicines, treatments, etc. |
| Food & nutrition: morning, afternoon, evening (with calories) … |
| Exercise: flexibility, cardio, resistance, sports … |
| Financial: |
| Infrastructure: home, transportation, |
| Appointments: |

To dos:	Accomplishments:

| Calls to make: |
| Correspondence: |
| Delegated, postponed, declined: |
| Evening rituals: dinner, family, bed … |
| Notes: search, look up, order … |

Journal:

Continuous Learning:

Day _____ Month _____ Day ___ Year _____

Day ____ Month _____ Day ___ Year _____

Spiritual: pray, praise, serve …
Family: love, listen, laugh …
Friends: reach out, encourage, share …
Morning rituals: shower, dress, breakfast …
Vitals: weight, blood pressure, etc.
Medical: medicines, treatments, etc.
Food & nutrition: morning, afternoon, evening (with calories) …
Exercise: flexibility, cardio, resistance, sports …
Financial:
Infrastructure: home, transportation,
Appointments:

To dos:	Accomplishments:

Calls to make:
Correspondence:
Delegated, postponed, declined:
Evening rituals: dinner, family, bed …
Notes: search, look up, order …

Journal:

Continuous Learning:

Day _____ Month _____ Day ___ Year _____

Day _____ Month _____ Day ___ Year _____

Spiritual: pray, praise, serve ...
Family: love, listen, laugh ...
Friends: reach out, encourage, share ...
Morning rituals: shower, dress, breakfast ...
Vitals: weight, blood pressure, etc.
Medical: medicines, treatments, etc.
Food & nutrition: morning, afternoon, evening (with calories) ...
Exercise: flexibility, cardio, resistance, sports ...
Financial:
Infrastructure: home, transportation,
Appointments:

To dos:	Accomplishments:

Calls to make:
Correspondence:
Delegated, postponed, declined:
Evening rituals: dinner, family, bed ...
Notes: search, look up, order ...
Journal:
Continuous Learning:

Day _____ Month _____ Day ___ Year _____

Day _____ Month _____ Day ___ Year _____

| Spiritual: pray, praise, serve … |
| Family: love, listen, laugh … |
| Friends: reach out, encourage, share … |
| Morning rituals: shower, dress, breakfast … |
| Vitals: weight, blood pressure, etc. |
| Medical: medicines, treatments, etc. |
| Food & nutrition: morning, afternoon, evening (with calories) … |
| Exercise: flexibility, cardio, resistance, sports … |
| Financial: |
| Infrastructure: home, transportation, |
| Appointments: |

To dos:	Accomplishments:

| Calls to make: |
| Correspondence: |
| Delegated, postponed, declined: |
| Evening rituals: dinner, family, bed … |
| Notes: search, look up, order … |

Journal:

Continuous Learning:

Day _____ Month _____ Day ___ Year _____

Day _____ Month _____ Day ____ Year _____

| Spiritual: pray, praise, serve ... |
| Family: love, listen, laugh ... |
| Friends: reach out, encourage, share ... |
| Morning rituals: shower, dress, breakfast ... |
| Vitals: weight, blood pressure, etc. |
| Medical: medicines, treatments, etc. |
| Food & nutrition: morning, afternoon, evening (with calories) ... |
| Exercise: flexibility, cardio, resistance, sports ... |
| Financial: |
| Infrastructure: home, transportation, |
| Appointments: |

To dos:	Accomplishments:

| Calls to make: |
| Correspondence: |
| Delegated, postponed, declined: |
| Evening rituals: dinner, family, bed ... |
| Notes: search, look up, order ... |

Journal:

Continuous Learning:

Day _____ Month _____ Day ___ Year _____

Day ____ Month _____ Day ___ Year _____

Spiritual: pray, praise, serve …	
Family: love, listen, laugh …	
Friends: reach out, encourage, share …	
Morning rituals: shower, dress, breakfast …	
Vitals: weight, blood pressure, etc.	
Medical: medicines, treatments, etc.	
Food & nutrition: morning, afternoon, evening (with calories) …	
Exercise: flexibility, cardio, resistance, sports …	
Financial:	
Infrastructure: home, transportation,	
Appointments:	

To dos:	Accomplishments:

Calls to make:

Correspondence:

Delegated, postponed, declined:

Evening rituals: dinner, family, bed …

Notes: search, look up, order …

Journal:

Continuous Learning:

Day _____ Month _____ Day ___ Year _____

Day _____ Month _____ Day ___ Year _____

Spiritual: pray, praise, serve ...
Family: love, listen, laugh ...
Friends: reach out, encourage, share ...
Morning rituals: shower, dress, breakfast ...
Vitals: weight, blood pressure, etc.
Medical: medicines, treatments, etc.
Food & nutrition: morning, afternoon, evening (with calories) ...
Exercise: flexibility, cardio, resistance, sports ...
Financial:
Infrastructure: home, transportation,
Appointments:

To dos:	Accomplishments:

Calls to make:
Correspondence:
Delegated, postponed, declined:
Evening rituals: dinner, family, bed ...
Notes: search, look up, order ...
Journal:
Continuous Learning:

Day _____ Month _____ Day ___ Year _____

Day _____ Month _____ Day ____ Year _____

Spiritual: pray, praise, serve …	
Family: love, listen, laugh …	
Friends: reach out, encourage, share …	
Morning rituals: shower, dress, breakfast …	
Vitals: weight, blood pressure, etc.	
Medical: medicines, treatments, etc.	
Food & nutrition: morning, afternoon, evening (with calories) …	
Exercise: flexibility, cardio, resistance, sports …	
Financial:	
Infrastructure: home, transportation,	
Appointments:	

To dos:	Accomplishments:

Calls to make:

Correspondence:

Delegated, postponed, declined:

Evening rituals: dinner, family, bed …

Notes: search, look up, order …

Journal:

Continuous Learning:

Day _____ Month _____ Day ___ Year _____

Day _____ Month _____ Day ___ Year _____

Spiritual: pray, praise, serve …	
Family: love, listen, laugh …	
Friends: reach out, encourage, share …	
Morning rituals: shower, dress, breakfast …	
Vitals: weight, blood pressure, etc.	
Medical: medicines, treatments, etc.	
Food & nutrition: morning, afternoon, evening (with calories) …	
Exercise: flexibility, cardio, resistance, sports …	
Financial:	
Infrastructure: home, transportation,	
Appointments:	

To dos:	Accomplishments:

Calls to make:

Correspondence:

Delegated, postponed, declined:

Evening rituals: dinner, family, bed …

Notes: search, look up, order …

Journal:

Continuous Learning:

Day _____ Month _____ Day ___ Year _____

Day _____ Month _____ Day ___ Year _____

| Spiritual: pray, praise, serve ... |
| Family: love, listen, laugh ... |
| Friends: reach out, encourage, share ... |
| Morning rituals: shower, dress, breakfast ... |
| Vitals: weight, blood pressure, etc. |
| Medical: medicines, treatments, etc. |
| Food & nutrition: morning, afternoon, evening (with calories) ... |
| Exercise: flexibility, cardio, resistance, sports ... |
| Financial: |
| Infrastructure: home, transportation, |
| Appointments: |

To dos:	Accomplishments:

| Calls to make: |
| Correspondence: |
| Delegated, postponed, declined: |
| Evening rituals: dinner, family, bed ... |
| Notes: search, look up, order ... |

Journal:

Continuous Learning:

Day _____ Month _____ Day ___ Year _____

Day _____ Month _____ Day ____ Year _____

| Spiritual: pray, praise, serve ... |
| Family: love, listen, laugh ... |
| Friends: reach out, encourage, share ... |
| Morning rituals: shower, dress, breakfast ... |
| Vitals: weight, blood pressure, etc. |
| Medical: medicines, treatments, etc. |
| Food & nutrition: morning, afternoon, evening (with calories) ... |
| Exercise: flexibility, cardio, resistance, sports ... |
| Financial: |
| Infrastructure: home, transportation, |
| Appointments: |

To dos:	Accomplishments:

| Calls to make: |
| Correspondence: |
| Delegated, postponed, declined: |
| Evening rituals: dinner, family, bed ... |
| Notes: search, look up, order ... |

Journal:

Continuous Learning:

Day _____ Month _____ Day ___ Year _____

Spiritual: pray, praise, serve ...	
Family: love, listen, laugh ...	
Friends: reach out, encourage, share ...	
Morning rituals: shower, dress, breakfast ...	
Vitals: weight, blood pressure, etc.	
Medical: medicines, treatments, etc.	
Food & nutrition: morning, afternoon, evening (with calories) ...	
Exercise: flexibility, cardio, resistance, sports ...	
Financial:	
Infrastructure: home, transportation,	
Appointments:	

To dos:	Accomplishments:

Calls to make:	
Correspondence:	
Delegated, postponed, declined:	
Evening rituals: dinner, family, bed ...	
Notes: search, look up, order ...	
Journal:	
Continuous Learning:	

Day _____ Month _____ Day ___ Year _____

Day _____ Month _____ Day ____ Year _____

Spiritual: pray, praise, serve …	
Family: love, listen, laugh …	
Friends: reach out, encourage, share …	
Morning rituals: shower, dress, breakfast …	
Vitals: weight, blood pressure, etc.	
Medical: medicines, treatments, etc.	
Food & nutrition: morning, afternoon, evening (with calories) …	
Exercise: flexibility, cardio, resistance, sports …	
Financial:	
Infrastructure: home, transportation,	
Appointments:	

To dos:	Accomplishments:

Calls to make:

Correspondence:

Delegated, postponed, declined:

Evening rituals: dinner, family, bed …

Notes: search, look up, order …

Journal:

Continuous Learning:

Day ____ Month _____ Day ___ Year _____

| Spiritual: pray, praise, serve … |
| Family: love, listen, laugh … |
| Friends: reach out, encourage, share … |
| Morning rituals: shower, dress, breakfast … |
| Vitals: weight, blood pressure, etc. |
| Medical: medicines, treatments, etc. |
| Food & nutrition: morning, afternoon, evening (with calories) … |
| Exercise: flexibility, cardio, resistance, sports … |
| Financial: |
| Infrastructure: home, transportation, |
| Appointments: |

To dos:	Accomplishments:

| Calls to make: |
| Correspondence: |
| Delegated, postponed, declined: |
| Evening rituals: dinner, family, bed … |
| Notes: search, look up, order … |

Journal:

Continuous Learning:

Day _____ Month _____ Day ___ Year _____

Day _____ Month _____ Day ___ Year _____

Spiritual: pray, praise, serve …
Family: love, listen, laugh …
Friends: reach out, encourage, share …
Morning rituals: shower, dress, breakfast …
Vitals: weight, blood pressure, etc.
Medical: medicines, treatments, etc.
Food & nutrition: morning, afternoon, evening (with calories) …
Exercise: flexibility, cardio, resistance, sports …
Financial:
Infrastructure: home, transportation,
Appointments:

To dos:	Accomplishments:

Calls to make:
Correspondence:
Delegated, postponed, declined:
Evening rituals: dinner, family, bed …
Notes: search, look up, order …

Journal:

Continuous Learning:

Day _____ Month _____ Day ___ Year _____

Day _____ Month _____ Day ____ Year _____

Spiritual: pray, praise, serve …	

Family: love, listen, laugh …

Friends: reach out, encourage, share …

Morning rituals: shower, dress, breakfast …

Vitals: weight, blood pressure, etc.

Medical: medicines, treatments, etc.

Food & nutrition: morning, afternoon, evening (with calories) …

Exercise: flexibility, cardio, resistance, sports …

Financial:

Infrastructure: home, transportation,

Appointments:

To dos:	Accomplishments:

Calls to make:

Correspondence:

Delegated, postponed, declined:

Evening rituals: dinner, family, bed …

Notes: search, look up, order …

Journal:

Continuous Learning:

Day _____ Month _____ Day ___ Year _____

Day _____ Month _____ Day ____ Year _____

| Spiritual: pray, praise, serve ... |
| Family: love, listen, laugh ... |
| Friends: reach out, encourage, share ... |
| Morning rituals: shower, dress, breakfast ... |
| Vitals: weight, blood pressure, etc. |
| Medical: medicines, treatments, etc. |
| Food & nutrition: morning, afternoon, evening (with calories) ... |
| Exercise: flexibility, cardio, resistance, sports ... |
| Financial: |
| Infrastructure: home, transportation, |
| Appointments: |

To dos:	Accomplishments:

| Calls to make: |
| Correspondence: |
| Delegated, postponed, declined: |
| Evening rituals: dinner, family, bed ... |
| Notes: search, look up, order ... |

Journal:

Continuous Learning:

Day _____ Month _____ Day ___ Year _____

·

Day _____ Month _____ Day ____ Year _____

| Spiritual: pray, praise, serve … |
| Family: love, listen, laugh … |
| Friends: reach out, encourage, share … |
| Morning rituals: shower, dress, breakfast … |
| Vitals: weight, blood pressure, etc. |
| Medical: medicines, treatments, etc. |
| Food & nutrition: morning, afternoon, evening (with calories) … |
| Exercise: flexibility, cardio, resistance, sports … |
| Financial: |
| Infrastructure: home, transportation, |
| Appointments: |

To dos:	Accomplishments:

| Calls to make: |
| Correspondence: |
| Delegated, postponed, declined: |
| Evening rituals: dinner, family, bed … |
| Notes: search, look up, order … |

Journal:

Continuous Learning:

Day _____ Month _____ Day ___ Year _____

Day _____ Month _____ Day ____ Year _____

Spiritual: pray, praise, serve …	
Family: love, listen, laugh …	
Friends: reach out, encourage, share …	
Morning rituals: shower, dress, breakfast …	
Vitals: weight, blood pressure, etc.	
Medical: medicines, treatments, etc.	
Food & nutrition: morning, afternoon, evening (with calories) …	
Exercise: flexibility, cardio, resistance, sports …	
Financial:	
Infrastructure: home, transportation,	
Appointments:	

To dos:	Accomplishments:

Calls to make:
Correspondence:
Delegated, postponed, declined:
Evening rituals: dinner, family, bed …
Notes: search, look up, order …

Journal:

Continuous Learning:

Day _____ Month _____ Day ___ Year _____

Day _____ Month _____ Day ____ Year _____

| Spiritual: pray, praise, serve … |
| Family: love, listen, laugh … |
| Friends: reach out, encourage, share … |
| Morning rituals: shower, dress, breakfast … |
| Vitals: weight, blood pressure, etc. |
| Medical: medicines, treatments, etc. |
| Food & nutrition: morning, afternoon, evening (with calories) … |
| Exercise: flexibility, cardio, resistance, sports … |
| Financial: |
| Infrastructure: home, transportation, |
| Appointments: |

To dos:	Accomplishments:

| Calls to make: |
| Correspondence: |
| Delegated, postponed, declined: |
| Evening rituals: dinner, family, bed … |
| Notes: search, look up, order … |

Journal:

Continuous Learning:

Day _____ Month _____ Day ____ Year _____

| Spiritual: pray, praise, serve … |
| Family: love, listen, laugh … |
| Friends: reach out, encourage, share … |
| Morning rituals: shower, dress, breakfast … |
| Vitals: weight, blood pressure, etc. |
| Medical: medicines, treatments, etc. |
| Food & nutrition: morning, afternoon, evening (with calories) … |
| Exercise: flexibility, cardio, resistance, sports … |
| Financial: |
| Infrastructure: home, transportation, |
| Appointments: |

To dos:	Accomplishments:

| Calls to make: |
| Correspondence: |
| Delegated, postponed, declined: |
| Evening rituals: dinner, family, bed … |
| Notes: search, look up, order … |

Journal:

Continuous Learning:

Day _____ Month _____ Day ___ Year _____

Spiritual: pray, praise, serve …
Family: love, listen, laugh …
Friends: reach out, encourage, share …
Morning rituals: shower, dress, breakfast …
Vitals: weight, blood pressure, etc.
Medical: medicines, treatments, etc.
Food & nutrition: morning, afternoon, evening (with calories) …
Exercise: flexibility, cardio, resistance, sports …
Financial:
Infrastructure: home, transportation,
Appointments:

To dos:	Accomplishments:

Calls to make:
Correspondence:
Delegated, postponed, declined:
Evening rituals: dinner, family, bed …
Notes: search, look up, order …

Journal:
Continuous Learning:

Day _____ Month _____ Day ___ Year _____

Spiritual: pray, praise, serve …	
Family: love, listen, laugh …	
Friends: reach out, encourage, share …	
Morning rituals: shower, dress, breakfast …	
Vitals: weight, blood pressure, etc.	
Medical: medicines, treatments, etc.	
Food & nutrition: morning, afternoon, evening (with calories) …	
Exercise: flexibility, cardio, resistance, sports …	
Financial:	
Infrastructure: home, transportation,	
Appointments:	

To dos:	Accomplishments:

Calls to make:

Correspondence:

Delegated, postponed, declined:

Evening rituals: dinner, family, bed …

Notes: search, look up, order …

Journal:

Continuous Learning:

Day _____ Month _____ Day ___ Year _____

Day _____ Month _____ Day ____ Year _____

Spiritual: pray, praise, serve ...
Family: love, listen, laugh ...
Friends: reach out, encourage, share ...
Morning rituals: shower, dress, breakfast ...
Vitals: weight, blood pressure, etc.
Medical: medicines, treatments, etc.
Food & nutrition: morning, afternoon, evening (with calories) ...
Exercise: flexibility, cardio, resistance, sports ...
Financial:
Infrastructure: home, transportation,
Appointments:

To dos:	Accomplishments:

Calls to make:
Correspondence:
Delegated, postponed, declined:
Evening rituals: dinner, family, bed ...
Notes: search, look up, order ...

Journal:

Continuous Learning:

Day _____ Month _____ Day ___ Year _____

Day _____ Month _____ Day _____ Year _____

Spiritual: pray, praise, serve …	
Family: love, listen, laugh …	
Friends: reach out, encourage, share …	
Morning rituals: shower, dress, breakfast …	
Vitals: weight, blood pressure, etc.	
Medical: medicines, treatments, etc.	
Food & nutrition: morning, afternoon, evening (with calories) …	
Exercise: flexibility, cardio, resistance, sports …	
Financial:	
Infrastructure: home, transportation,	
Appointments:	

To dos:	Accomplishments:

Calls to make:

Correspondence:

Delegated, postponed, declined:

Evening rituals: dinner, family, bed …

Notes: search, look up, order …

Journal:

Continuous Learning:

Day _____ Month _____ Day ___ Year _____

Day _____ Month _____ Day ____ Year _____

Spiritual: pray, praise, serve ...	
Family: love, listen, laugh ...	
Friends: reach out, encourage, share ...	
Morning rituals: shower, dress, breakfast ...	
Vitals: weight, blood pressure, etc.	
Medical: medicines, treatments, etc.	
Food & nutrition: morning, afternoon, evening (with calories) ...	
Exercise: flexibility, cardio, resistance, sports ...	
Financial:	
Infrastructure: home, transportation,	
Appointments:	

To dos:	Accomplishments:

Calls to make:

Correspondence:

Delegated, postponed, declined:

Evening rituals: dinner, family, bed ...

Notes: search, look up, order ...

Journal:

Continuous Learning:

Day _____ Month _____ Day ___ Year _____

Day _____ Month _____ Day ___ Year _____

Spiritual: pray, praise, serve ...

Family: love, listen, laugh ...

Friends: reach out, encourage, share ...

Morning rituals: shower, dress, breakfast ...

Vitals: weight, blood pressure, etc.

Medical: medicines, treatments, etc.

Food & nutrition: morning, afternoon, evening (with calories) ...

Exercise: flexibility, cardio, resistance, sports ...

Financial:

Infrastructure: home, transportation,

Appointments:

To dos:	Accomplishments:

Calls to make:

Correspondence:

Delegated, postponed, declined:

Evening rituals: dinner, family, bed ...

Notes: search, look up, order ...

Journal:

Continuous Learning:

Day _____ Month _____ Day ___ Year _____

Day _____ Month _____ Day ____ Year _____

| Spiritual: pray, praise, serve … |
| Family: love, listen, laugh … |
| Friends: reach out, encourage, share … |
| Morning rituals: shower, dress, breakfast … |
| Vitals: weight, blood pressure, etc. |
| Medical: medicines, treatments, etc. |
| Food & nutrition: morning, afternoon, evening (with calories) … |
| Exercise: flexibility, cardio, resistance, sports … |
| Financial: |
| Infrastructure: home, transportation, |
| Appointments: |

To dos:	Accomplishments:

| Calls to make: |
| Correspondence: |
| Delegated, postponed, declined: |
| Evening rituals: dinner, family, bed … |
| Notes: search, look up, order … |

Journal:

Continuous Learning:

Day _____ Month _____ Day ___ Year _____

The Business Model Canvas

Designed for: Designed by:

Key Partners	Key Activities	Value Propositions	Customer Relationships	Customer Segments
	Key Resources		**Channels**	

Cost Structure

Revenue Streams

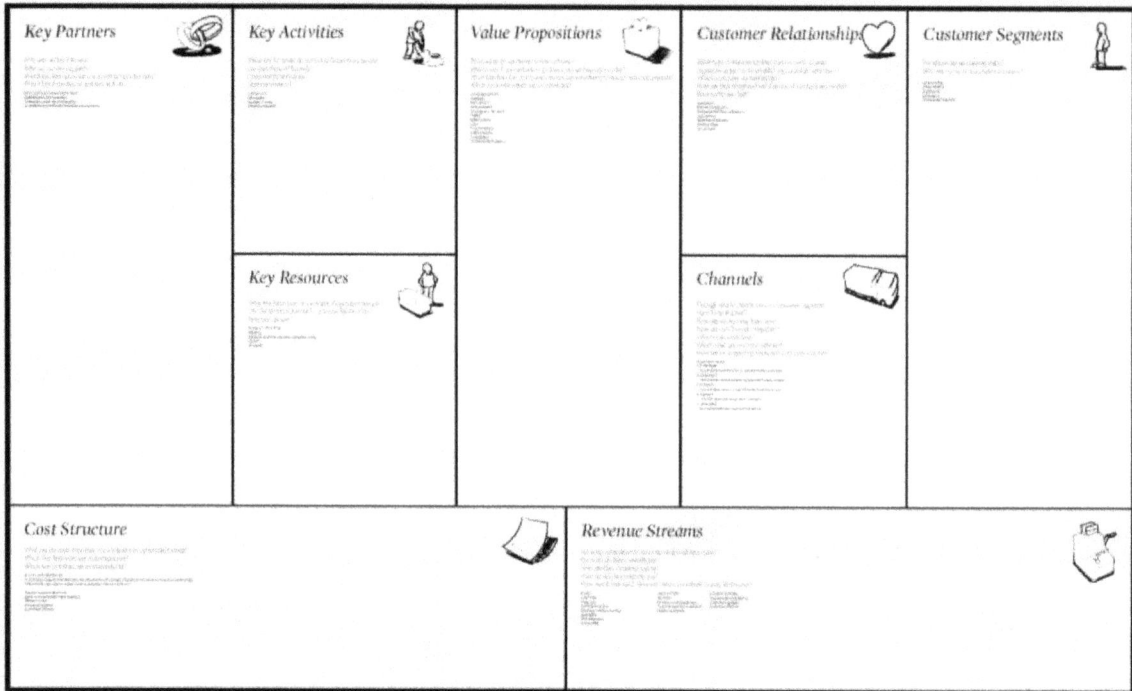

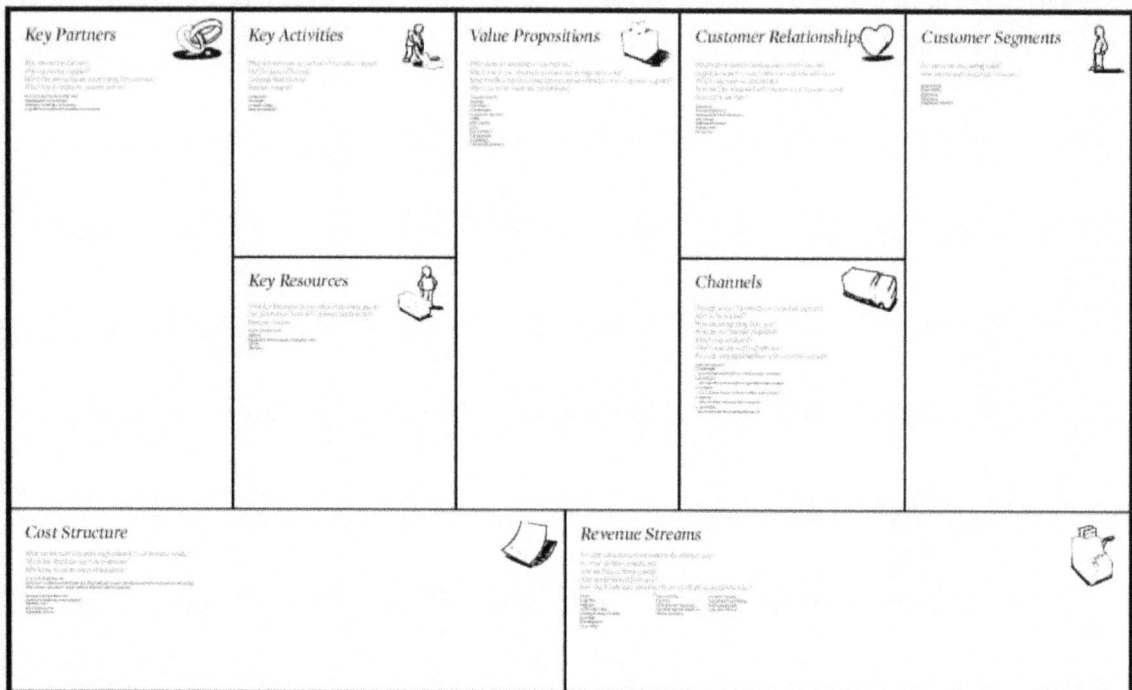

www.businessmodelgeneration.com

The Business Model Canvas

Designed for: Designed by:

Key Partners	Key Activities	Value Propositions	Customer Relationships	Customer Segments
	Key Resources		**Channels**	

Cost Structure

Revenue Streams

www.businessmodelgeneration.com

Figure 1. The Business Model Canvas

Day _____ Month _____ Day ____ Year _____

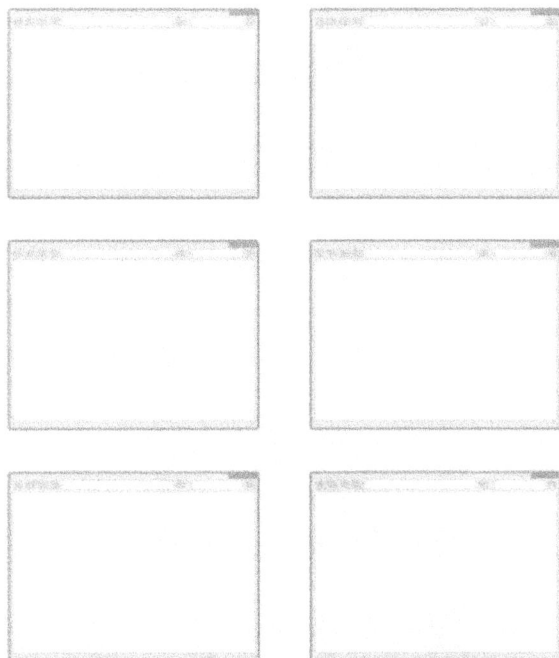

Page:

Project:

Client:

Author

Notes

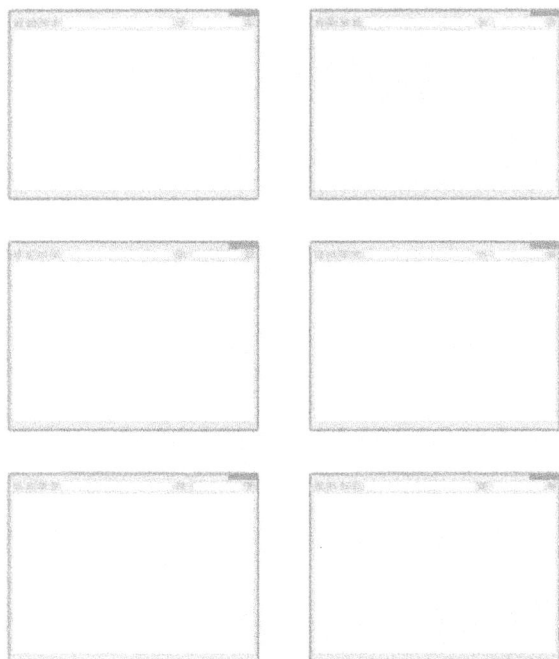

Page:

Project:

Client:

Author

Notes.

Figure 2. Storyboard templates.

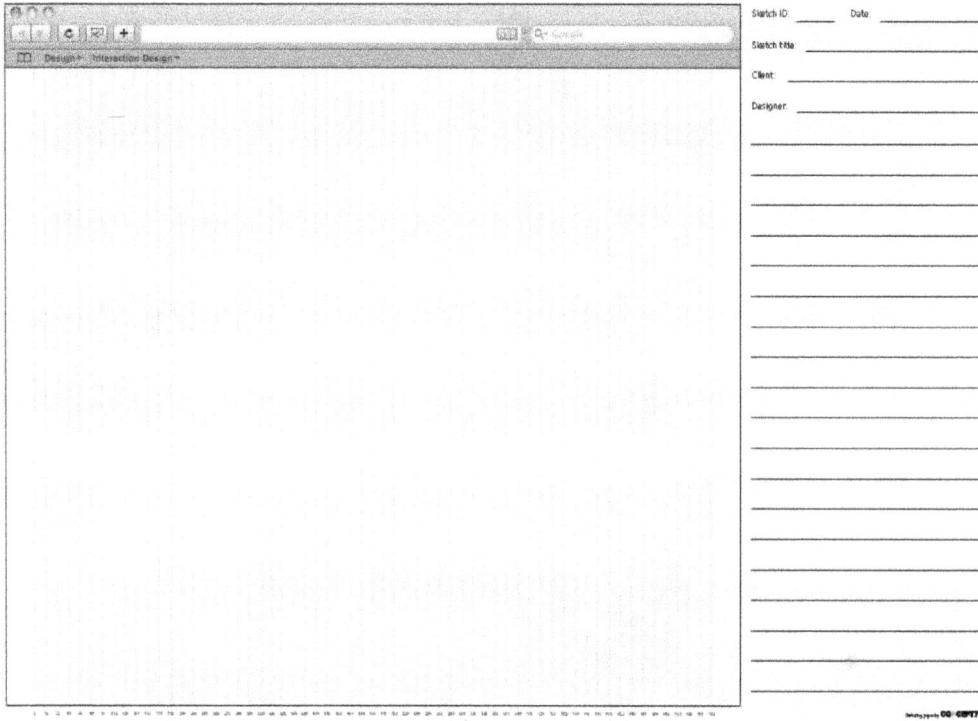

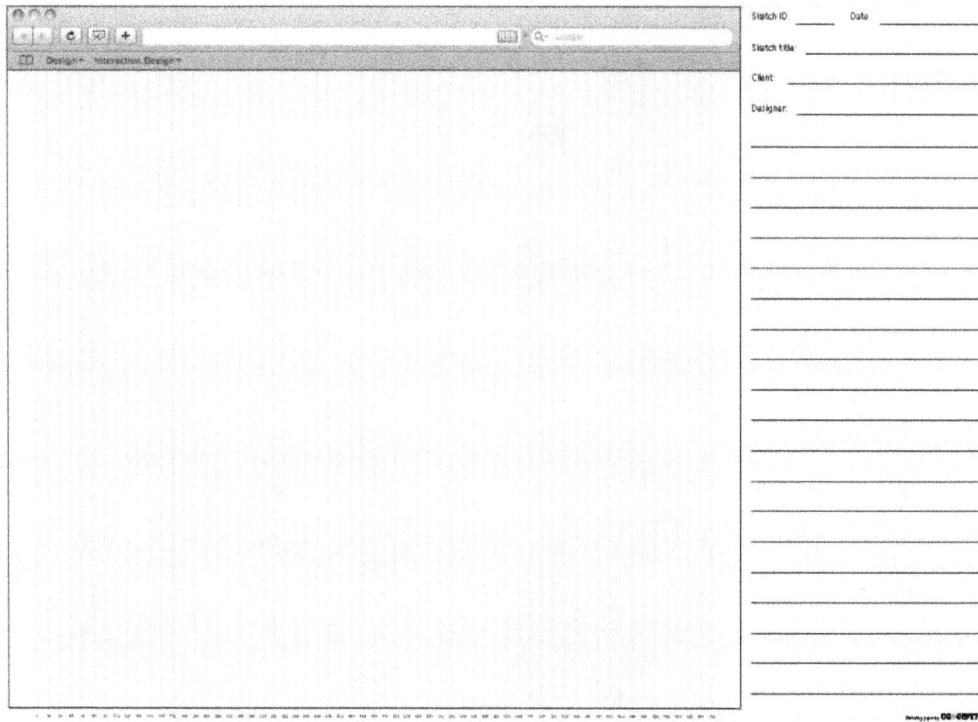

Figure 3. Browser sketch pad.

Day ____ Month _____ Day ___ Year _____

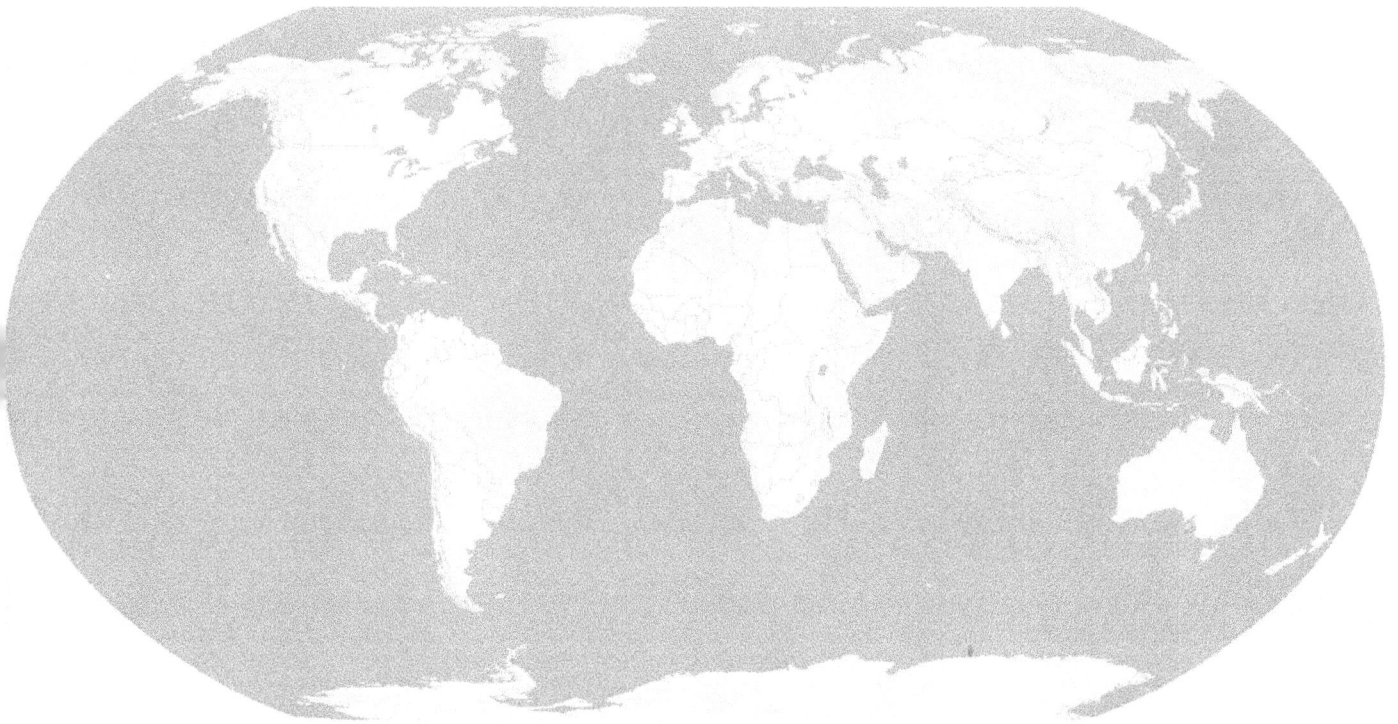

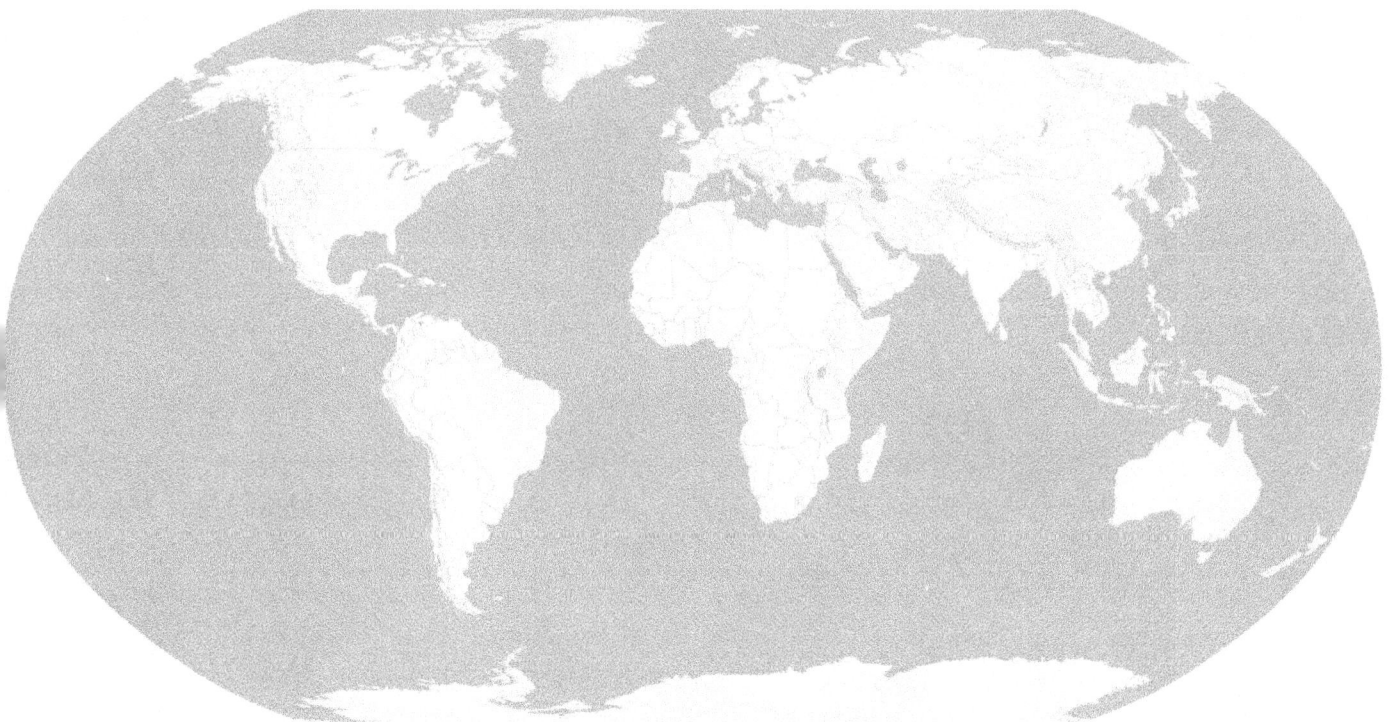

Figure 4. Robinson projection of Empty World.